Ellen Reid

D0534076

TELEPHONE COURTESY & CUSTOMER SERVICE

REVISED EDITION

Lloyd Finch

CRISP PUBLICATIONS, INC.
Los Altos, California

TELEPHONE COURTESY & CUSTOMER SERVICE

REVISED EDITION

Lloyd Finch

CREDITS
Editor: **Michael Crisp**
Designer: **Carol Harris**
Typesetting: **Interface Studio**
Cover Design: **Carol Harris**
Artwork: **Ralph Mapson**

All rights reserved. No part of this book may be reproduced or transmitted in any form or by any means now known or to be invented, electronic or mechanical, including photocopying, recording, or by any information storage or retrieval system without written permission from the author or publisher, except for the brief inclusion of quotations in a review.

Copyright © 1987, 1990 by Crisp Publications, Inc.
Printed in the United States of America

English language Crisp books are distributed worldwide. Our major international distributors include:

CANADA: Reid Publishing, LTD., Box 7267, Oakville, Ontario Canada L6J 6L6. TEL: (416) 842-4428, FAX: (416) 842-9327

AUSTRALIA: Career Builders, P. O. Box 1051, Springwood, Brisbane, Queensland, Australia 4127. TEL: 841-1061, FAX: 841-1580

NEW ZEALAND: Career Builders, P. O. Box 571, Manurewa, Auckland, New Zealand. TEL: 266-5276, FAX: 266-4152

JAPAN: Phoenix Associates Co., Mizuho Bldg. 2-12-2, Kami Osaki, Shinagawa-Ku, Tokyo 141, Japan. TEL: 3-443-7231, FAX: 3-443-7640

Selected Crisp titles are also available in other languages. Contact International Rights Manager Tim Polk at (415) 949-4888 for more information.

Library of Congress Catalog Card Number 90-82869
Finch, Lloyd
Telephone Courtesy & Customer Service
ISBN 1-56052-064-7

PREFACE

Welcome to **Telephone Courtesy and Customer Service.** You have been selected for this training because your manager feels you are an important provider of customer service for your organization.

This book has been written so that you can complete it in a relatively short time. The important thing is to read the material carefully, understand it, and apply it to your job.

There are four sections in this book. **Section I** provides objectives for the reader, defines a quality customer service provider and discusses service responsibility. **Section II** discusses telephone techniques and their importance to providing quality service. **Section III** explains customer "wants and needs" and describes the importance of a positive attitude. **Section IV** teaches the reader how to manage "customer perceptions."

Keep this book near your work location for reference. By using it regularly you will learn correct telephone techniques and develop the personal skills required to provide the best possible customer service.

Applying the telephone customer service skills in this book will help you become a professional provider of quality customer service. This should be your objective.

Get out your pencil, relax and enjoy this book.

Lloyd Finch

NOTE: Two excellent videos have been produced by the author based on the material in this book. They are: *Effective Call Management* and *Managing Difficult Customers.* For more information, call Crisp Publications, Inc. at (415) 949-4888.

TELEPHONE COURTESY & CUSTOMER SERVICE is divided into four sections. Each section is designed to help you progress toward the goal
of providing quality customer service when using the telephone.

The objective of each section is:

Section I	—	To understand the basics of providing high quality customer service.
Section II	—	To learn proper telephone techniques.
Section III	—	To understand the customer.
Section IV	—	To manage the customer's perception and understand the essential role customer service plays in the success of your company.

The four objectives are interrelated. Good customer service cannot be provided until all four are understood and applied.

Being a professional customer service provider (regardless of your title or position) is an essential key to the ultimate success of any organization. This makes you a very important person.

CONTENTS

Preface i
Section I Quality Customer Service 2
Customer Service Is Everyone's Responsibility 3
The Importance Of The Telephone In Your Organization 4
Section II Proper Telephone Techniques 6
1. Handling The Telephone 7
2. Your Voice Inflection 9
3. Your Best Voice 10
4. Addressing The Caller 12
5. Answering The Telephone 13
6. Effective Listening 14
7. Managing Objections 16
8. The Art Of Negotiation 19
9. The Service Follow-Up Call 23
10. Asking Questions 24
11. Making The Outbound Service Call 30
12. Delivering Bad News 31
13. Managing Different Caller Behaviors 32
14. Managing Your Voice Message System 36
15. Managing Telephone Messages 37
16. Managing The Customer Callback 38
17. Some Statements To Avoid 39
18. Closing The Conversation 43
Section III Understanding Customer Needs 45
What Your Customer Wants 47
Attitude Is Your Key To Success 52
Quality Customer Service Defined 57
Section IV Managing The Customer's Perception 58
Case Study: The Wholesale Widget Company 59
The Customer's Perception: An Exercise 61
The Customer Service Call 64
Your Telephone Service Skills Inventory 67
Your Action Plan for Better Service 68

SECTION I

QUALITY CUSTOMER SERVICE

Quality customer service is provided by a person like you. A quality customer service provider is a person who:

1. ACCEPTS RESPONSIBILITY FOR PROVIDING TIMELY CUSTOMER SERVICE IN A COURTEOUS MANNER.

2. UNDERSTANDS THAT THE SUCCESS OF AN ORGANIZATION DEPENDS ON GOOD CUSTOMER SERVICE.

3. LEARNS AND PRACTICES CUSTOMER SERVICE SKILLS IN A POSITIVE MANNER.

Often employees are so busy there is little time to think about their jobs or how they relate to the overall success of the company. Sometimes, those who spend much of their day on the telephone talking with outsiders don't consider their jobs to be very important. The fact is that anyone regularly involved with customer contact has one of the most important jobs in that organization. Following are some points to consider:

- THE SUCCESS OF A COMPANY DEPENDS ON CUSTOMERS. THESE CUSTOMERS WILL NOT RETURN UNLESS THEY ARE TREATED PROFESSIONALLY COURTEOUSLY.

- MANAGERS NORMALLY TALK WITH ONLY A FEW CUSTOMERS EACH WEEK. OTHER EMPLOYEES TALK WITH DOZENS EACH DAY.

- ANYONE WORKING DIRECTLY WITH CUSTOMERS OCCUPIES A POSITION OF TRUST.

- COMPANIES WITH REPUTATIONS FOR OUTSTANDING SERVICE WERE BUILT OVER TIME BY PEOPLE LIKE YOU.

CUSTOMER SERVICE IS EVERYONE'S RESPONSIBILITY

When we think about customer service, it is common to think that certain individuals or departments are the only ones responsible for providing that service. However, in most organizations customer service departments represent only a portion of the overall service responsibility. Everyone from president to clerk provides customer service and contributes to a company's reputation for service and courtesy.

If all employees learned to provide the service concepts presented in this book, that company's reputation with customers would be considered "excellent."

In the next few pages, you will learn about telephone techniques to help you become more professional when you are on the phone with customers and clients.

Learning good techniques and skills is essential but not as important as applying what has been learned on a daily basis.

QUESTION: DAVE IS A LOBBY RECEPTIONIST FOR ACME SYSTEMS INC. HIS RESPONSIBILITIES INCLUDE REGISTERING AND PROVIDING SECURITY BADGES FOR ALL NON-EMPLOYEES WHO ENTER THE BUILDING. IS DAVE RESPONSIBLE FOR CUSTOMER SERVICE?

ANSWER: YOU BET!

THE IMPORTANCE OF THE TELEPHONE IN YOUR ORGANIZATION

Think for a moment about the role of the telephone where you work. Chances are it would be difficult to conduct business without it. Although there are salespeople and other representatives who meet face to face with customers to generate business, the telephone is probably responsible for most customer contacts.

On an average day, do you know what portion of your customers receive service over the telephone as compared to contact in person by a representative of your company? Although companies differ, it is not unusual to have more than 80 percent of customer contact provided by telephone.

If your company's primary customer contact is by telephone, do you know who is primarily responsible for the company's customer service reputation? (check one)

☐ Those who meet face to face with the customer

☐ Those who talk with customers on the telephone

☐ Managers and supervisors

The best answer is those who use the telephone.

Who is responsible for providing good customer service? (check all that apply)

☐ me ☐ the managers ☐ the sales department

☐ officers of the company ☐ our telephone receptionists

☐ our clerks ☐ the delivery people ☐ our outside service people

☐ the technical support staff ☐ others

If you checked all of the choices, you get an "A." The most important check mark, however, belongs next to the word "me"!

DIAGRAM OF A QUALITY CONSCIOUS COMPANY

The diagram below illustrates how a customer is viewed by the best customer service companies.

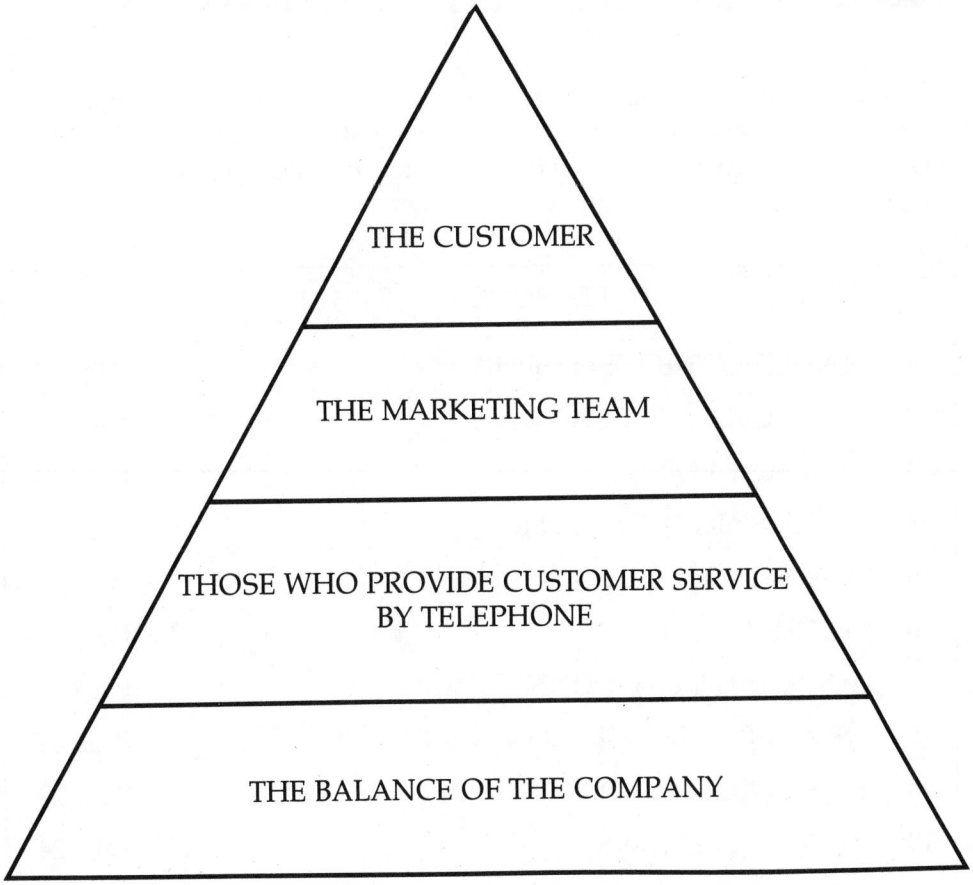

Please notice that customers are at the top of the PYRAMID but supported by marketing and sales and dependent on the rest of the company to give them the attention they deserve. Keep this diagram in mind as you learn about telephone techniques that can help provide quality customer service.

SECTION II

PROPER TELEPHONE TECHNIQUES

Proper telephone techniques are essential to provide quality customer service. In the following pages you will learn eighteen important telephone techniques. How effectively you use them is up to you.

TELEPHONE TECHNIQUES

1. HANDLING THE TELEPHONE — Page 7
2. YOUR VOICE INFLECTION — Page 9
3. YOUR BEST VOICE — Page 10
4. ADDRESSING THE CALLER — Page 12
5. ANSWERING THE TELEPHONE — Page 13
6. EFFECTIVE LISTENING — Page 14
7. MANAGING OBJECTIONS — Page 16
8. THE ART OF NEGOTIATION — Page 19
9. THE SERVICE FOLLOW-UP CALL — Page 23
10. ASKING QUESTIONS — Page 24
11. MAKING THE OUTBOUND SERVICE CALL — Page 30
12. DELIVERING BAD NEWS — Page 31
13. MANAGING DIFFERENT CALLER BEHAVIORS — Page 32
14. MANAGING YOUR VOICE MESSAGE SYSTEM — Page 36
15. MANAGING TELEPHONE MESSAGES — Page 37
16. MANAGING THE CUSTOMER CALLBACK — Page 38
17. SOME STATEMENTS TO AVOID — Page 39
18. CLOSING THE CONVERSATION — Page 43

TELEPHONE TECHNIQUE ONE: HANDLING THE TELEPHONE

Features of the telephone need to be understood. These features are designed to help you handle calls smoothly. At first glance they may seem complicated but normally are easy to use. To understand the capabilities of your telephone better, read about the available features or ask a more experienced person to explain them to you. Then practice until they become automatic.

> Joan needed to transfer a caller to a co-worker. She wasn't sure how to do it. After quickly reading the instructions Joan made the transfer. The caller was disconnected. If Joan had spent a few minutes practicing the call transfer feature, the disconnect would not have occurred.

- The time to learn about your telephone is ahead of time. Don't practice on the caller. Be familiar with all of the features.
- Hold the transmitter portion of the telephone directly in front of your mouth. If the transmitter is held away from your mouth, you risk not being understood.

> Keep in mind that speaking on the telephone requires better articulation than is necessary in face-to-face conversations.

- Place the telephone on your desk so the receiver will be picked up without banging into anything. No one likes unnecessary noise.
- Avoid side conversations while talking on the telephone. Your party deserves your full attention. Do not attempt to carry on two conversations at the same time.

HANDLING THE TELEPHONE (continued)

► Make sure the caller is placed on hold before discussing his or her situation with a co-worker.

> Wouldn't it be embarassing if you told a co-worker that a caller didn't sound too smart, only to discover that he/she was listening?

► Never eat or drink while talking. If your mouth is full when the telephone rings, wait a few seconds before answering.

► Answer in as few rings as possible. A maximum of three rings is a good standard.

> Some organizations have a "three-ring policy." Check to see if yours does.

► When you place a caller on hold to answer another line, ask for permission and WAIT FOR AN ANSWER.

> **EXAMPLE:** "Would you mind holding while I answer my other line?" Wait for the customer to say, "Sure go ahead." Too often you hear, "please hold" and the person is gone.

► If you have several callers on hold, remember the priority of each call. If necessary, make notes of who is holding and on which line.

> Nothing is more irritating than to answer the question, "Whom are your holding for?" several times.

TELEPHONE TECHNIQUE TWO: YOUR VOICE INFLECTION

Try this inflection exercise by speaking into a tape recorder.

Read the following sentence in your normal voice:

"Jimmy didn't show up for work this morning."

Now restate the same sentence with surprise in your voice.

Try it again, but this time make it a casual statement.

Next, make it sound like a secret.

Finally, turn it into a question.

If done properly, as your inflection changes, the sentence will convey a completely different meaning to the listener.

TELEPHONE TECHNIQUE THREE: YOUR BEST VOICE

We all have voices that sound different. Some of us have the deep voice of authority, while others of us sound meek or frail. Voices can be pleasant or annoying, easy to decipher or unintelligible, clear as a bell or squeaky. The voice you project is determined by four factors, all of which can be controlled.

ENERGY—The energy in your voice reflects your attitude and enthusiasm.

RATE OF SPEECH—A normal rate is 125 words a minute. Speaking faster can create problems.

PITCH—This can be a monotone, a low or a high pitch. Ideally you should vary your tone and inflection.

QUALITY—The above three factors make up your voice quality.

There are several things you can do to produce a more desirable speaking voice. Some include:

1. Warm up by humming a song. This will help deepen the sound of your voice.

2. Practicing your pitch and control by calling a telephone recording device and delivering several messages. Then listen to the playback and critique yourself or ask a friend to help.

3. Role play with a friend and tape record the conversation. Review it for tone, rate of delivery, etc.

4. Take a speech class in a local college or extension program to learn some voice exercises to help you avoid a monotone sound.

5. PUT A SMILE INTO YOUR VOICE. It's easy to do. Simply remember to smile as you answer a call. Believe it or not, your voice will sound friendlier.

VOICE SELF-ASSESSMENT

Your voice reflects your personality. If it needs improvement, you can do it, but you must be willing to try. Practicing voice techniques is no different than practicing a sport. If you stay at it, you're bound to improve.

Rate your voice using the following self-evaluation. Check those characteristics that apply to you, and then ask a friend to help evaluate your responses.

MY VOICE:

DESIRABLE TRAITS		UNDESIRABLE TRAITS	
is pleasant-sounding	____	is nasal	____
has pitch variations	____	sounds throaty	____
has a normal rate	____	is raspy	____
varies in volume	____	sometimes squeaks	____
has distinct articulation	____	is a boring monotone	____
sounds like I am smiling	____	is too weak	____
has ample force	____	is too loud	____
stresses proper accents	____	has too many pauses	____
		does not convey a "smile"	____

For any undesirable traits checked, you should begin work on correcting them. The techniques suggested in this book should help, but you may also need to enroll in a speech improvement class so an expert can diagnose and prescribe appropriate voice exercises.

TELEPHONE TECHNIQUE FOUR: ADDRESSING THE CALLER

Rules about how to address callers can be confusing because of the many options. Therefore, the following may help.

There are seven basic ways to address a calling party.

Mr. Mrs. Miss Ms. First Name Sir and Ma'am

The average caller may or may not be sensitive about how he or she is addressed. To be on the safe side, keep these suggestions in mind:

1. When addressing a male, you are always correct to use Mr. or Sir.

2. Addressing a woman is more confusing. The use of Mrs. or Miss is common and generally acceptable. Some women prefer Ms. and may request this form of address. If you are uncertain, simply ask the caller for her preference. (Shall I address you as Miss or Mrs? Is it Mrs. or Miss? Is it Miss or Ms. Taylor?)

3. Often when you ask for the correct form of address the caller will suggest the use of a first name. The use of the customer's first name is then acceptable. Use of a first name may also be acceptable (but not always) when:

   - You have established a good rapport over a period of time.

   - You have been called by your first name.

   - You know the caller and know he/she is comfortable with a first name basis.

TELEPHONE TECHNIQUE FIVE: ANSWERING THE TELEPHONE

A caller will mentally begin to measure the quality of the organization before they hear a voice by the number of rings it takes to get an answer. The next impression comes with the first voice they hear. Imagine a cheerful "Good Morning, Jones Enterprises" verus a terse, clipped "International Widget, please hold."

The rules for answering a telephone are simple but they need to be continually reviewed and practiced. Following are the most basic ones, which should always be employed.

1. Use the four answering courtesies:
   - Greet the caller
   - State your organization (or department)
   - Introduce yourself
   - Offer your help

EXAMPLE: GOOD AFTERNOON, ACCOUNTING, MARY JONES SPEAKING. HOW MAY I HELP YOU?

2. Be enthusiastic when you answer. Help make the calling party feel truly welcome.

A TIRED, VOICE LACKING IN ENTHUSIASM IS UNAPPEALING.

3. Use friendly phrases as part of your greeting.

SUCH AS: THANKS FOR CALLING. MAY I HELP YOU? HOW ARE YOU TODAY?

4. Remember to smile as you pick up the receiver.

IDEA: TAPE THE WORD SMILE ON YOUR RECEIVER

TELEPHONE TECHNIQUE SIX: EFFECTIVE LISTENING

The first lesson in listening is to be aware that there are only three types of expressions you hear from callers. Callers will:

1. MAKE STATEMENTS
2. OFFER OBJECTIONS or
3. ASK QUESTIONS

Similarly, there are three things that can happen when you fail to listen closely.

1. YOU WILL HEAR WHAT YOU WANT TO HEAR
2. YOU WILL HEAR WHAT YOU EXPECT TO HEAR
3. YOU WILL NOT RECOGNIZE THE DIFFERENCE BETWEEN A STATEMENT, OBJECTION OR QUESTION.

If you do not listen closely, you may not be able to understand what the call is about. For example:

CUSTOMER STATEMENT: "YOUR PRICES ARE A LITTLE HIGHER THAN I THOUGHT THEY WOULD BE."

Close your eyes and imagine a customer making this remark. How would you interpret it?
(check one)

____ THE CUSTOMER HAS AN OBJECTION.

____ THE CUSTOMER MADE A STATEMENT.

____ THE CUSTOMER HAS ASKED A QUESTION.

Answer: The customer was making a statement

EFFECTIVE LISTENING (Continued)

Let's see how Helen, a professional service representative, would respond to the statement on the previous page.

CUSTOMER:	"YOUR PRICES ARE A LITTLE HIGHER THAN I THOUGHT THEY WOULD BE."
HELEN:	"I HOPE THAT WON'T BE A PROBLEM. THEY ARE EXCELLENT PRODUCTS. MAY I HAVE YOUR BILLING ADDRESS?"

Helen acknowledged the statement and then moved the conversation to the next step. If Helen had not been listening closely, she might have misinterpreted the statement as an objection or a question. For example, suppose Helen had interpreted the customer's statement as an objection. Her response might have gone like this.

CUSTOMER:	"YOUR PRICES ARE A LITTLE HIGHER THAN I THOUGHT THEY WOULD BE."
HELEN:	"OUR PRICES ARE VERY COMPETITIVE. IN FACT, WE LOWERED SOME PRICES THIS YEAR."
CUSTOMER:	"THEY SEEM HIGH TO ME."
HELEN:	"IF YOU COMPARED OUR PRICES WITH OUR COMPETITORS, YOU WOULD FIND THAT ON THE AVERAGE WE ARE VERY COMPETITIVE."
CUSTOMER:	"WHO ARE YOUR MAJOR COMPETITORS?"

In this example, Helen allowed the conversation to become a discussion regarding prices and competitors. Helen lost control simply because she handled a statement as if it were an objection.

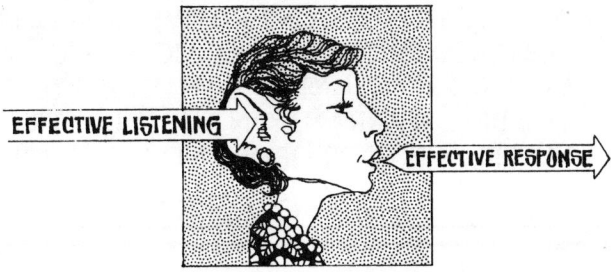

TELEPHONE TECHNIQUE SEVEN: MANAGING OBJECTIONS

An objection occurs when the caller is opposed to the proposed plan of action. When you hear an objection, it is important to address it immediately. If the caller offers an objection and you ignore it, you may have lost a customer.

EXAMPLE:

CUSTOMER:	(OBJECTION) "YOUR PRICES SEEM HIGH AND I THINK I SHOULD SHOP AROUND AND COMPARE PRICES BEFORE I PLACE MY ORDER."
DOUG:	"I AM SURE THAT YOU WILL BE SATISFIED WITH OUR PRODUCT. WILL A FRIDAY DELIVERY DATE BE OKAY?"

In this example Doug was not listening. He did not hear the customer's objection and as a result tried to move the sale along. Doug deserves credit for trying to get the order but there is not much point when the customer's objection goes unanswered.

Most of us do not like objections. We sometimes think that if objections are ignored they will go away. They won't. Objections require an immediate reply.

EXAMPLE:

CUSTOMER:	(OBJECTION) "I THINK I SHOULD COMPARE PRICES BEFORE PLACING AN ORDER."
HELEN:	"THAT'S FINE. OUR CUSTOMERS TELL US WE ARE VERY PRICE COMPETITIVE. WE RECENTLY LOWERED PRICES ON THE MODEL YOU ARE CONSIDERING, AND IT CONTINUES TO CARRY THE BEST WARRANTY IN THE INDUSTRY. IF YOU PLACE YOUR ORDER NOW, WE COULD DELIVER IT EARLY NEXT WEEK."

MANAGING OBJECTIONS (Continued)

If you ignore objections or questions, a caller will usually:

1. Stop you and repeat the objection or the question.

2. Not say anything to you but still be dissatisfied because you ignored them.

When listening always pay attention to voice inflection. It communicates a great deal. Suppose the customer says, ''Your delivery dates are unbelievable.'' If the customer made this statement in an assertive voice, you would interpret it as an objection. If delivered in a cheerful voice, the customer has probably paid a compliment. Callers will let you know when they object to something, and their objections will usually be direct and to the point. Your job is to listen closely.

SUMMARY: MANAGING OBJECTIONS

1. Listen to what the caller says.

2. Always provide an immediate response.

3. State the response in clear and positive terms.

4. Do not provide unnecessary information and conversation.

On the following page is an exercise to help you learn to distinguish between statements, questions and objections. This activity should help you to become a more sensitive listener.

STATEMENTS, QUESTIONS OR OBJECTIONS

In the following exercise read each expression as if it has just been delivered to you on the telephone. Then write an "S" if you think it is a STATEMENT, a "Q" if you think it is a QUESTION and an "O" for those you think are OBJECTIONS. For expressions that are both questions and objections, write both letters in order of your ranking.

Assume all responses have been made in a normal tone of voice (you will notice that all punctuation has purposely been left out).

1. ____ I THINK YOUR SERVICE IS QUITE GOOD
2. ____ YOUR DELIVERY DATES ARE CERTAINLY LONG ENOUGH
3. ____ WHY DOES THE BILL SHOW $107.00
4. ____ YOUR PRICES ARE JUST TOO HIGH FOR ME
5. ____ YOU DON'T UNDERSTAND. I NEED SOMEONE OUT HERE TODAY
6. ____ WHEN WILL IT BE IN STOCK
7. ____ WHAT ARE YOU GOING TO DO ABOUT THE BACK ORDER
8. ____ I CAN'T WAIT. I NEED TO TALK WITH HER TODAY
9. ____ WHY IS HE NEVER AROUND WHEN I NEED HIM
10. ____ I AM NOT GOING TO PAY THAT BILL

(Answers are at the bottom of this page)

ANSWERS:

1. STATEMENT
2. OBJECTION, STATEMENT
3. QUESTION
4. OBJECTION
5. OBJECTION
6. QUESTION
7. QUESTION
8. OBJECTION
9. OBJECTION, STATEMENT
10. OBJECTION

TELEPHONE TECHNIQUE EIGHT: THE ART OF NEGOTIATION*

Often you will have to negotiate with a customer. Negotiating involves recognizing the needs of the caller, comparing them against your organization's ability to deliver what is required and then reaching a solution that will satisfy both parties. Negotiation is required when a request is made for service you cannot or do not offer.

Negotiation begins with "ACTION ISSUES." These are concerns or requests that need to be met in order to satisfy the caller.

Successful negotiation does not mean offering a service your company cannot provide. Instead it means the ability to reach a compromise that is acceptable to both your organization and the caller.

To illustrate some negotiation techniques, let's listen in on a conversation between Jane and a customer.

CUSTOMER:	"This is Bob Martin calling. I must speak with Mrs. Sims right now."
JANE:	"I'm sorry, sir, but she is on another call. May I help you or take your telephone number and have her call you back?"
CUSTOMER:	"No, I can't wait. Interrupt her and let her know that I must speak to her."

Jane has an assertive customer who is demanding to talk with Mrs. Sims.

Jane knows that Mrs. Sims is already on an important call and does not want to be interrupted.

In this situation there is a conflict between what the customer wants and what Jane can provide. Usually in this type of situation there is room for negotiation.

If you were confronted with this situation what would you do to provide a compromise the customer would accept?

* For an excellent book on negotiation order *Successful Negotiations* from the back of the book.

THE ART OF NEGOTIATION (Continued)

HERE ARE SOME TIPS:

1. Ask questions to determine the problem.

2. When you select a course of action, be direct and specific in your statements.

3. Remain positive and service oriented.

If you were Jane, how would you respond to the customer?

THE CUSTOMER SAYS: "No, I can't wait. Interrupt and let her know that I must speak to her."

Write your response. (Keep the above guideline in mind.)

YOUR RESPONSE: _____

_____

_____

_____

_____

_____

_____

(Read the facing page to see how Jane negotiated with the customer.)

CUSTOMER: "NO, I CAN'T WAIT. INTERRUPT AND LET HER KNOW THAT I MUST SPEAK WITH HER."

JANE: "SIR, I'M SURE MRS. SIMS WOULD LIKE TO TALK TO YOU, BUT SINCE SHE IS NOT AVAILABLE, PLEASE EXPLAIN WHAT YOU NEED AND I'LL EITHER PERSONALLY TAKE CARE OF IT OR FIND SOMEONE TO HELP YOU. WILL THAT BE ALL RIGHT?"

CUSTOMER: "WELL, MAYBE YOU CAN HELP. OUR SYSTEM HAS BEEN DOWN FOR ABOUT TWO HOURS."

JANE: "DID YOU CALL OUR SERVICE DEPARTMENT?"

CUSTOMER: "YES I DID."

JANE: "WHAT DID THEY SAY?"

CUSTOMER: "ONE OF YOUR TECHNICIANS WAS TO HAVE BEEN HERE BY TEN O'CLOCK. HE HAS NOT SHOWN UP. I CAN'T REACH YOUR SERVICE DEPARTMENT BECAUSE THE LINES ARE CONSTANTLY BUSY."

JANE: "I'LL CALL THE SERVICE DEPARTMENT AND FIND OUT WHAT THEY ARE DOING ABOUT YOUR PROBLEM. WILL YOU HOLD FOR A MOMENT?"

CUSTOMER: "OKAY."

(JANE CALLS THE SERVICE DEPARTMENT AND LEARNS THE TECHNICIAN WAS DELAYED AT ANOTHER LOCATION AND WILL NOT BE AT MR. MARTIN'S FOR ANOTHER HOUR.)

JANE: "MR. MARTIN, I TALKED WITH THE SUPERVISOR IN THE CUSTOMER SERVICE DEPARTMENT AND SHE SAID YOUR TECHNICIAN HAS BEEN DELAYED BUT WILL BE THERE WITHIN THE HOUR. I WILL CHECK BACK REGULARLY TO MAKE CERTAIN THE TECHNICIAN WILL GO DIRECTLY TO YOUR COMPANY TO MEET HIS NEW DEADLINE. I WILL ALSO INFORM MRS. SIMS THAT YOU CALLED. WILL THAT BE ALL RIGHT?"

CUSTOMER: "I GUESS SO."

JANE: "THANKS FOR YOUR PATIENCE, MR. MARTIN."

CUSTOMER: "OKAY, THANKS FOR YOUR HELP."

THE ART OF NEGOTIATION (Continued)

REVIEW

Obviously, the customer is not completely satisfied. He would like the technician to be at his business immediately, but since this is not possible, an alternate plan was arranged and he has agreed to it. Let's review Jane's course of action.

1. She raised her voice slightly to become more assertive.

2. By asking questions, she learned what the customer needed.

3. She proposed a course of action.

4. She was direct and specific in her statements.

In most service situations, an acceptable compromise can be reached through negotiation. Since you control the service, you are in a position to suggest a compromise or make another arrangement. Jane had two ACTION ISSUES to cope with.

The customer demanded to speak with Mrs. Sims.

The customer wanted a technician immediately.

Jane knew Mrs. Sims was not available. She also knew she would not be able to get the technician to the customer's location immediately. Despite this, she took positive action, presented a plan and asked that the customer accept it.

When you control service you must be careful with your statements to avoid coming on too strong. Even though you cannot always provide what the customer wants, it is important to deliver the response in a courteous manner.

TELEPHONE TECHNIQUE NINE: THE SERVICE FOLLOW-UP CALL

Following up on the service you provide is professional. In the situation you just read, Jane or Mrs. Sims should follow up with Mr. Martin to see if he is satisfied. Many customer service providers do not regularly follow up. They claim they do not have time. Even when it is impossible to follow up with every customer, there are certain situations where it should be done. A few examples include:

1. NOTHING WENT RIGHT. Sometimes you have a situation in which, despite everyone's best effort, nothing goes right. Once the problems have been corrected the customer should be called to determine whether everything is now satisfactory. The customer will usually appreciate this courtesy.

2. THE IRATE CUSTOMER. When you hang up from a conversation with an irate customer, the last thing you want to do is speak with that customer again. Whether the cause of the complaint was legitimate or questionable, a follow-up call is a good idea. By calling to ask if the action you initiated was satisfactory, the customer will be pleasantly surprised to hear from you and perhaps will become a good customer.

3. A NEW CUSTOMER. When you establish a new account or provide service to a new customer, it's a good time to extend an extra courtesy. Make a follow-up call to learn if everything is satisfactory. The customer's perception of your company will be enhanced, and repeat business may be likely.

4. THE REGULAR CUSTOMER. Those who do business with you deserve occasional follow-up calls. It is easy to take regular customers for granted. An occasional friendly follow-up service call tells regular customers "we care about you."

Never hesitate to make a follow-up service call. Even when the customer was irate or the service you provided did not go as planned, call. It is always better to know the level of customer satisfaction than guess at it. If a customer continues to have a problem, you need to know about it so it can be corrected. If there is no longer a problem, the customer will appreciate the follow-up.

TELEPHONE TECHNIQUE TEN: ASKING QUESTIONS

Often you are required to ask questions to get information you need. There are two types of questions that can be used and each has a particular purpose. The types are open questions and closed questions.

OPEN QUESTIONS ARE DESIGNED TO OBTAIN ANSWERS THAT CANNOT BE ANSWERED WITH A SIMPLE YES OR NO.

FOR EXAMPLE, IF YOU ASK A CUSTOMER, ''DID YOU RECEIVE THE SHIPMENT?''

THE ANSWER WILL BE EITHER YES OR NO.

IF YOU WANTED THE CUSTOMER TO DISCUSS THE PARTICULARS OF THE SHIPMENT, YOU COULD ASK INSTEAD:

''WHAT WAS THE CONDITION OF THE SHIPMENT WHEN IT ARRIVED?''

AN EXPLANATION IS REQUIRED.

Use OPEN questions when you want a customer to explain or discuss something. CLOSED questions should be used when all you need is a yes or no. Use both types of questions to gain better control of your telephone contacts. It is also possible to shorten telephone calls by effectively using OPEN and CLOSED questions.

At the beginning of most customer calls you need to learn what the customer wants, so you would use OPEN questions. Later, you may need to employ CLOSED questions to get the customer's agreement, to understand a service request or just to manage the conversation and your time.

Open questions begin with the words:
How, Why, When, Who, What, and Where

EXAMPLES OF OPEN QUESTIONS:
- HOW OFTEN DOES THAT HAPPEN?
- WHAT DID YOU DO BEFORE THE PROBLEM STARTED?
- WHO IS RESPONSIBLE FOR YOUR BILLING?
- WHEN DID THE PACKAGE ARRIVE?

Closed questions begin with words like:
Did, Can, Have, Do, Is, Will, and Would

EXAMPLES OF CLOSED QUESTIONS:
- DID YOU CALL THEM?
- DO YOU HAVE YOUR BILL?
- HAVE YOU RECEIVED OUR REFUND?
- WILL YOU ATTEND OUR SEMINAR?
- MAY I DO THAT FOR YOU?

Any statement can be "closed" by following it with a question. For example:

I WOULD LIKE TO SEND YOU A BROCHURE ABOUT OUR PRODUCTS. WILL THAT BE OKAY?

YOU PROMISED TO CALL ME BACK BY FOUR O'CLOCK. IS THAT CORRECT?

Other examples of closed questions you can use at the end of statements include:

DO YOU APPROVE?
WILL YOU PARTICIPATE?
IS THAT A GOOD TIME TO CALL?
WILL THAT BE ALL RIGHT?

List some of your own in the space below:

_____

_____

_____

_____

ASKING QUESTIONS (Continued)

Short closed questions can also be used to obtain the customer's agreement. For example:

> OUR TECHNICIAN WILL BE THERE ON FRIDAY.
> WILL THAT BE OKAY?
>
> WE HAVE TO BILL YOU FOR THAT SERVICE. IS THAT ALL RIGHT?
>
> I WILL CALL YOU 10:00 AM MONDAY MORNING.
> WILL YOU BE AVAILABLE?

These examples sound like you are giving the customer a choice. However, you are basically asking for a confirmation of your statement.

Suppose you were arranging an appointment for one of your sales representatives. The only open date you had to offer was Tuesday at nine o'clock. You could say:

> "I'M SORRY, MISS JOHNSON, BUT THE ONLY DATE MR. STEVENS HAS OPEN IS TUESDAY AT NINE O'CLOCK. I HOPE THAT WILL BE OKAY."

This statement is poorly phrased. It could be stated more positively if you said:

> "MISS JOHNSON, I HAVE ARRANGED FOR OUR SALES REPRESENTATIVE MR. STEVENS TO VISIT YOU ON TUESDAY AT NINE O'CLOCK. WILL THAT BE ALL RIGHT?

The customer might still request a different date; however, your statement sounds like you have taken positive action.

Take a few minutes to complete the following exercise on OPEN and CLOSED questions. Identify the questions below as either CLOSED or OPEN. Write a C for CLOSED questions and an O for the OPEN ones. Answers are on the next page.

1. ____ What did you do with the disk?
2. ____ Where did the customer's paperwork go?
3. ____ Have you paid the bill?
4. ____ We need the payment by Friday. Will that be okay?
5. ____ How much work is required?
6. ____ Can it be fixed?
7. ____ Is the customer holding?
8. ____ How many calls did we make today?
9. ____ Why did our incoming calls stop at three o'clock?
10. ____ Ms. Jones is happy with our service. Isn't she?
11. ____ Why didn't you test it?
12. ____ Will you call me?
13. ____ How long have you been doing business with us?
14. ____ Do you want to have lunch?
15. ____ Customers are always right. Aren't they?
16. ____ Did the boss tell you to do that?
17. ____ What is the latest inventory level?
18. ____ They were pretty high. Weren't they?
19. ____ Closed questions are answered with a yes or no. Isn't that true?
20. ____ Why do open questions begin with words like how, why, when, where and what?

ASKING QUESTIONS (continued)

(Answers from page 27)

QUESTION	ANSWER
1. OPEN	QUESTION BEGINS WITH WHAT
2. OPEN	QUESTION BEGINS WITH WHERE
3. CLOSED	QUESTION BEGINS WITH HAVE
4. CLOSED	ENDS WITH A CLOSED QUESTION
5. OPEN	QUESTION BEGINS WITH HOW
6. CLOSED	QUESTION BEGINS WITH CAN
7. CLOSED	QUESTION BEGINS WITH IS
8. OPEN	QUESTION BEGINS WITH HOW
9. OPEN	QUESTION BEGINS WITH WHY
10. CLOSED	ENDS WITH A CLOSED QUESTION
11. OPEN	QUESTION BEGINS WITH WHY
12. CLOSED	QUESTION BEGINS WITH WILL
13. OPEN	QUESTION BEGINS WITH HOW
14. CLOSED	QUESTION BEGINS WITH DO
15. CLOSED	ENDS WITH A CLOSED QUESTION
16. CLOSED	QUESTION BEGINS WITH DID
17. OPEN	QUESTION BEGINS WITH WHAT
18. CLOSED	ENDS WITH A CLOSED QUESTION
19. CLOSED	ENDS WITH A CLOSED QUESTION
20. OPEN	QUESTION BEGINS WITH WHY

KEY WORDS	
OPEN	**CLOSED**
HOW	DID
WHY	CAN
WHEN	HAVE
WHO	DO
WHAT	WILL
WHERE	IS
	WOULD

To improve your use of open and closed questions, practice is required. Don't you agree? (closed)

USING QUESTIONS WHEN FACT FINDING

When fact finding, keep the following in mind. It will help you determine when to use OPEN or CLOSED questions. You may wish to copy this page and keep it near your phone to remind you when to use OPEN or CLOSED questions.

1. TO DETERMINE PROBLEMS, UNDERSTAND REQUESTS OR ESTABLISH NEEDS

(USE OPEN QUESTIONS)

2. TO ASK CALLERS TO EXPLAIN REQUESTS OR PROBLEMS

(USE OPEN QUESTIONS)

3. TO ASK FOR MORE INFORMATION TO DETERMINE A COURSE OF ACTION

(USE BOTH OPEN AND CLOSED QUESTIONS)

4. TO GET AGREEMENT

(USE CLOSED QUESTIONS)

SUSAN'S PROBLEM: SUSAN WORKS IN THE MESSSAGE CENTER OF THE COAST CITY BANK. SHE HAS RECEIVED SEVERAL COMPLAINTS ABOUT THE LACK OF INFORMATION SHE OBTAINS FROM CUSTOMERS IN THE MESSAGES SHE TAKES FOR OTHERS. SUSAN COULD IMPROVE HER PERFORMANCE IF SHE FOLLOWED THE ADVICE ABOVE. DON'T YOU AGREE?

TELEPHONE TECHNIQUE ELEVEN: MAKING THE OUTBOUND SERVICE CALL

Anytime you call a customer there are important steps to follow. Even though you may not be calling to sell a product, the basic steps of a successful telemarketing call still apply.

BEFORE YOU MAKE YOUR CALL, DEVELOP AN ACTION PLAN.

- GREET THE CUSTOMER IN A FRIENDLY WAY
- INTRODUCE YOURSELF AND YOUR COMPANY
- STATE THE PURPOSE OF THE CALL
- DELIVER YOUR MESSAGE IN FRIENDLY, CLEAR AND BUSINESS-LIKE TERMS, LEAVING ROOM FOR QUESTIONS
- STATE ANY CUSTOMER BENEFITS
- ASK FOR AGREEMENT

Here's an example:

Cindy mistakenly overbooked a seminar. She needed to call Mrs. Stanger from the Acme Company to explain why the seminar date had to be changed. Cindy developed the following telemarketing action plan.

HER OBJECTIVE: Arrange a new seminar date for the Acme Company.

THE APPROACH: Briefly explain the need for the change and offer two alternate dates.

CUSTOMER BENEFITS: The seminar will be less crowded on the new dates and Acme will receive more attention from the seminar leader.

Cindy called Mrs. Stanger and said: "Good morning, Mrs. Stanger. This is Cindy Rogers from GAC. How are you today?...The reason for my call is to discuss your seminar date. The date I booked for your group is too crowded. What I can do is offer a date that will be less crowded. This means you will be able to ask more questions and receive more attention from the seminar leader. I have the 16th or 20th available. Do you have a preference?

In the situation above, Cindy did a good job because she turned a negative situation positive by planning ahead.

TELEPHONE TECHNIQUE TWELVE: DELIVERING BAD NEWS

Occasionally you will not be able to provide that which was promised. In these situations it is essential to telephone the customer to explain what has happened. Keeping a customer informed is courteous service. There will be times when it may be unpleasant to deliver bad news but it must be done.

There are two approaches you can use. We call one the DIRECT APPROACH and the other GOOD NEWS/BAD NEWS.

HERE IS AN EXAMPLE OF THE DIRECT APPROACH:

> "Good morning, Mr. King. This is Jim West from Woodwinds Unlimited. Do you have a moment? The reason for my call is to let you know that I made a mistake when I added your bill yesterday. I quoted you $287.00 but the correct total is $337.00. I apologize for the error but wanted to insure the correct amount was okay with you."

HERE IS THE SAME EXAMPLE USING THE GOOD NEWS/BAD NEWS APPROACH

> "Good morning Mr. King. This is Jim West from Woodwinds Unlimited. How are you today? I wanted you to know that I confirmed our technician will visit you on Friday as scheduled. I also wanted you to know that I misquoted the service charge during our last conversation. I quoted a service charge of $125.00 and it's really $150.00. I apologize for the error and hope it won't cause problems."

When you make an error (and we all do), it is important to accept responsibility for it. Be honest with your customer. No one likes unpleasant surprises such as unexpected billing amounts, people who do not show up or shipments that differ from what was ordered.

TELEPHONE TECHNIQUE THIRTEEN: MANAGING DIFFERENT CALLER BEHAVIORS

Every caller is different. Experienced customer service providers learn to recognize these differences and adjust their responses accordingly in order to provide better service.

Let's look at four different types of caller behavior often heard on the telephone.

CALLER BEHAVIOR PATTERNS

1. Assertive/Demanding
2. Angry
3. Passive
4. Talkative

MANAGING THE CONVERSATION WITH AN ASSERTIVE/DEMANDING CUSTOMER

Assertive/demanding people are pretty easy to recognize on the telephone because they are quick to show authority, demand action, and usually get to the point immediately. There is seldom any mystery as to what they want because they make it clear. They spend little time with social or other non-business conversation. Their calls will generally be shorter than most because they want to get business taken care of. Does this mean they are upset or angry? No. However, it is easy to mistake their assertiveness for anger, especially if you fail to listen closely.

When dealing with a demanding customer on the telephone you may need to raise your assertiveness level to simply manage the conversation.

How to raise your assertiveness level.

1. If your voice is soft raise it slightly.
2. Be direct and to the point in your statements.
3. Keep the non-business conversation to a minimum.

A word of caution: Keep your assertiveness level just below the callers. Matching the customers assertiveness could produce an argument.

A final point, do not be offended by a lack of rapport with this type of customer. Remember, they are interested in the business side not the social or relationship side of business.

SUMMARY: HOW TO RESPOND TO AN ASSERTIVE/DEMANDING CALLER

1. Listen so that you will understand the problem or request.
2. Match some of the customer's assertiveness.
3. Use closed questions to help control the conversation.
4. Be friendly, but specific and direct in your statements.
5. Remain courteous.

MANAGING THE ANGRY CALLER

Angry customers are a challenge even to the most experienced customer service provider. The task can be difficult but also very rewarding especially when an angry customer calms down and actually becomes friendly.

When you have telephone contact with an irate customer there are three important techniques that will help you manage the conversation.

1. LISTEN—so you will understand the problem or concern
2. RELATE—apologize in a general way or in a broad sense
3. PROPOSE AN ACTION PLAN—that will solve the problem

EXAMPLES: How to Relate

> "Mrs Smiley, I understand how you must feel."
>
> "I'm sorry about the confusion."
>
> "Mr. Welch, I don't blame you for being upset. Let's see if we can correct the problem."

Note that in the above examples the apology is very general. You can always apologize for the situation or the confusion, etc. . . . without admitting that you or your company were wrong. Most customers will find the "general" apology acceptable.

When the customer has a legitimate complaint sometimes it's best to relate by agreeing.

EXAMPLES:

> "Mrs. Johnson, you're right. You were promised a callback yesterday and we didn't call. Let's start again and get this problem solved."
>
> "I'm sorry Mr. Valdez, I promised you delivery by yesterday and didn't make it. This time I promise we'll do it right."

When a customer complains, offer your concern that they are upset, but do not take aggressive or hostile comments personally. Often an angry caller will display a lot of emotion. When this happens, do your best to remain calm and avoid getting caught up in the emotion.

Finally, once you have, listen closely and relate it's time to offer an action plan. Make sure your action plan is one you can deliver. The action plan should be stated in clear and concise terms.

EXAMPLES:

> "I'll check with accounting and call you back with an answer before 4:00 o'clock today."
>
> "Let's do this. I'll call the technician and find out what time you can expect her and then I'll call you. Will that be all right?"

MANAGING DIFFERENT CALLER BEHAVIORS (Continued)

SUMMARY: TELEPHONE TECHNIQUES FOR MANAGING THE ANGRY CUSTOMER

1. Listen closely so you will understand the problem.
2. Relate by apologizing in a general way or in a broad sense.
3. Propose an action plan and then do it!
4. Stay calm and avoid getting involved in the customer's emotion.
5. Remain courteous.

THE PASSIVE CUSTOMER

Passive customers are usually easy to manage and service. Satisfied customers are often passive. Experience has told them they do not need to push or complain. They know they will receive the service they need.

One mistake frequently made with passive customers is to take them for granted. Because they usually don't complain we assume they are satisfied with the service received. It is not the nature of most passive people to demand service or to express anger. If they are dissatisfied with your service they may simply quit calling.

Jenny's supervisor asked her why the activity had dropped off on the Hodges Company account. Jenny said she wasn't sure why Mr. Hodges had quit calling. According to Jenny; "I think Mr. Hodges was very pleased with our service. He never complained, even when we had computer problems and his bills were incorrect he didn't say a word about it."

One technique that is usually successful with passive customers is to periodically ask them about your level of service.

EXAMPLE:

Jenny could have asked: "Mr. Hodges, I know your billing was incorrect last month but we have that fixed now. Have there been any other problems?"

Sometimes the passive customer may need a little prompting.

EXAMPLE:

Mr. "Hodges, according to my records your shipments have been on time. Have there been any problems?"

MANAGING THE TALKATIVE CALLER

Talkative people are often interesting and enjoyable, but on the telephone they can take up a lot of time. To avoid losing valuable time, a conversation with a talkative customer must be managed. There are three proven techniques that will work for you.

1. Ask closed questions
2. Use space control
3. Provide minimal response

CLOSED QUESTIONS

Use closed questions as often as possible with a talkative caller. The short answers you receive will help move the conversation along. Ask open questions only when you need more explanation. (See page 24 for more on closed and open questions.)

SPACE CONTROL

Space control sounds exotic but it simply means provide little space between your statements for the talkative customer to interrupt. You can do this and remain courteous without rushing. Between sentences use a shorter pause than normal and then immediately make your next statement or ask a question.

MINIMAL RESPONSE

Do not invite unnecessary conversation. The talkative customer may want to engage you in non-business conversation. To reduce the amount of conversation keep your response to a minimum and always steer the conversation back to business.

MINIMAL RESPONSE EXAMPLES:

CUSTOMER: How is everything going? Have they been keeping you busy?

JENNY: We have been real busy. *How may I help you?*

CUSTOMER: Hi, Jenny! This is Mike. How's everything going? Did you watch the movie on cable last night?

JENNY: Hi, Mike. No, I missed the movie but I heard it was good. *What can I do for you?*

TELEPHONE TECHNIQUE FOURTEEN: MANAGING YOUR VOICE MESSAGING SYSTEM

Voice messaging systems are designed to improve office productivity. However, they can be a problem when used improperly. One common problem is some people, when assigned an electronic mailbox, quit answering their phone. The intent of the system is just the opposite. Answer your telephone when you are at your desk and not on the telephone and let the system pick it up when you can't answer.

Here's a few other common courtesies that apply to voice messaging.

1. Upon returning to your desk, check for messages. Return calls promptly.

2. When returning a call and the system answers, leave a clear and detailed message including your mailbox number. One idea behind a messaging system is the privacy it provides and therefore more detailed and longer messages can be left.

3. As your schedule changes, the greeting you leave in your mailbox should also change. For example, if you are going to be away from your desk for a few hours, leave a message stating when you will return. When gone for longer periods, call forward your calls to someone who can help the caller or leave instructions within your greeting stating who is taking your calls and how they can be reached.

4. Understand the features of your voice messaging system. Booklets are usually available explaining what is available. Your system administrator can answer more detailed questions.

Robert did not understand the voice messaging system very well. He thought he left a personal message for a friend on the other side of the office. By mistake he selected a broadcast code instead of the friend's mailbox number. Now everyone knows what the message says.

TELEPHONE TECHNIQUE FIFTEEN: MANAGING TELEPHONE MESSAGES

When you manage a volume of incoming calls or are away from your desk, telephone messages often pile up. If there are many messages, priorities need to be established and to do so requires organization on your part, especially when there is limited time in which to return these calls.

Determining in what order calls should be returned is an important decision. For example, suppose you had eight messages.

The messages were:
1. Customer John Stanley called twice. He says it's urgent.
2. Your friend Michelle called.
3. Customer R. Bliss called. He has some questions.
4. Customer Joyce Smith called. Has an order to place.
5. Mike from accounting called. Has a question.
6. Ron called. Please confirm your report will be in by Tuesday.
7. Mrs. Davis called. Has a question regarding the company picnic.
8. Customer Jim Oates called. Must speak with you ASAP.

The Comparison Method

One easy method of determining message priority is quickly comparing one message to another. For example: Is message #1 (John Stanley) more or less important than message #2 (Michelle's call)? Next compare message #1 to message #3 and decide if it is more or less important. By continuing the process the correct decisions will be reached.

Initially this process may take a few minutes, but with a little experience it can be done quickly just by glancing at each message.

Using the comparison method, in what order would you return the above calls? (Write in the number of the message.)

1. _____ 5. _____
2. _____ 6. _____
3. _____ 7. _____
4. _____

Check your answers with the author's (shown below).

ANSWERS:

1. 1	5. 5	If your answers are close to these you
2. 8	6. 6	are on the right track. Messages
3. 4	7. 7	1 and 8 were selected 1 & 2
4. 3	8. 2	because they are urgent.

TELEPHONE TECHNIQUE SIXTEEN: MANAGING THE CUSTOMER CALLBACK

When you are unable to handle a request at the time of the original telephone call, here are four callback steps to follow:

1. BRIEFLY EXPLAIN THE NEED FOR THE CALLBACK.

2. ASK FOR PERMISSION TO MAKE A CALLBACK.

3. MAKE A COMMITMENT TO CALL AT AN AGREED UPON TIME.

4. PERSONALIZE YOUR STATEMENTS.

Here is an example of how to manage a customer callback:

> "IT WILL TAKE SOME TIME TO GET THAT INFORMATION FOR YOU, MR. JONES. WILL IT BE OKAY IF I CALL YOU BACK THIS AFTERNOON BEFORE FOUR O'CLOCK?"

If we break this statement into the four callback steps, it would look like this:

> **1.** It will take some time **(explaining the need for the callback)** to get that information for you, **2.** Mr. Jones. **(personalized) 3.** Will it be okay **(asking permission)** if I call you back this afternoon **4.** before four o'clock? **(commitment)**

Another example:

> "Mrs. Jones, it's going to take a while because I want to research the material completely for you. I won't be able to call you back until tomorrow morning at 10:00 am. Will that be all right?"

Remember, customers expect a fast response. When you cannot provide one, you need to commit to an action plan, including the time you will call back. Be sure to offer a return call time that you can meet. Don't compound your problem by committing to an unrealistic deadline.

TELEPHONE TECHNIQUE SEVENTEEN: SOME STATEMENTS TO AVOID

Often unknowingly, employees make a telephone statement that will leave customers with negative perceptions. Following are some of those common telephone statements.

(CHECK THOSE STATEMENTS YOU HAVE HEARD OR USED YOURSELF)

1. ____ I'm sorry. Mrs. Jones is still at lunch.
2. ____ I don't know where he is, may I take your number and have him call you?
3. ____ I think she is still having coffee. I'll have her call you.
4. ____ She is in the middle of a big customer problem. Would you like to leave a message?
5. ____ He is at the doctor's office.
6. ____ She went home early.
7. ____ I'm sorry Mr. Smith has not come in yet.
8. ____ The service person should be there on Friday.
9. ____ Your bill should be correct now.
10. ____ Our service department takes forever to answer the phone.

The next page contains an evaluation of these ''too common'' statements.

SOME STATEMENTS TO AVOID (Continued)

1. "I'm sorry. Mrs. Jones is still at lunch."
The key word is "still." Saying "still" implies a long lunch hour.

2. "I don't know where he is. May I take your number and have him call you?"
You hear this a lot. When there is a call for someone and you are not sure where the person is, that information should not be shared with the caller. A simple "He is unavailable at the moment. May I have him call you?" will do fine.

3. "I think she is still having coffee. I'll have her call you."
Similar to question one and two. This information need not be shared with the customer.

4. "She is in the middle of a big customer problem."
This statement tells your caller that you have "big customer problems." Why share this type of information? Simply say, "I'm sorry she is unavailable," and offer to take a message or to help the caller.

5. "He is at the doctor's office."
Do not share personal information about a co-worker with the customer. Instead, say "He will be out of the office until three o'clock. May I help you?"

6. "She went home early."
Customers get furious at this one. They need help and discover the person who can help them went home early. Treat this situation as personal information and do not share it.

7. "I'm sorry but Mr. Smith has not come in yet."
The word "yet" implies being late. Just say: "I am sorry but Mr. Smith is not available. May I help you?"

8. "Our service person should be there on Friday."
Keep statements positive. Avoid creating doubts about your service. Change "should be there" to "will be there."

9. "Your bill should be correct now."
Words like "should" as compared to "will" make your statement negative. Use positive words.

10. "The service department takes forever to answer the phone."
If you have internal problems, it is not a good idea to share the situation with your caller. Don't broadcast problems.

There are other negative telephone statements that are frequently used. You can probably list several. The point is, everything you say on the telephone influences a caller's perception of you *and* your company.

On the facing page is a short exercise asking you to convert "negative customer statements" into "positive customer statements."

Read the following statements. If you think the statement might result in a poor customer perception of your company, rewrite it. Here's a tip. Imagine you are a customer hearing the statement during a call. Compare your answers with those of the author on the next page.

1. "THE SHIPPING DATE ON YOUR ORDER SHOULD BE NEXT FRIDAY."

_____

_____

2. "I'M SORRY I DIDN'T CALL YOU BACK. MY BOSS HAD US IN ANOTHER MEETING THAT LASTED ALL MORNING."

_____

_____

3. "I HOPE THIS WILL SOLVE YOUR PROBLEM."

_____

_____

4. "I DON'T UNDERSTAND WHY CUSTOMER SERVICE DIDN'T HELP YOU."

_____

_____

5. "ORDER PROCESSING HAS HAD A LOT OF PROBLEMS LATELY. I'LL CALL OVER THERE AND GET THIS STRAIGHTENED OUT FOR YOU."

_____

_____

6. "MR. KING IS IN A MEETING. WHY DON'T YOU CALL BACK IN AN HOUR?"

_____

_____

7. "I'M SORRY IT TOOK SO LONG. NOW WHAT DO YOU WANT?"

_____

_____

8. "I'M SORRY YOU HAD TO WAIT. OUR TELEPHONE OPERATORS ARE VERY SLOW."

_____

_____

SOME STATEMENTS TO AVOID (Continued)

(ANSWERS FROM PAGE 41)

Your phrasing does not have to be identical with the following suggestions. If your statement is positive, it is probably correct.

1. "THE SHIPPING DATE ON YOUR ORDER SHOULD BE NEXT FRIDAY."
"Your shipping date will be next Friday."

2. "I'M SORRY I DIDN'T CALL YOU BACK. MY BOSS HAD US IN ANOTHER MEETING THAT LASTED ALL MORNING."
"I'm sorry I was unable to get back to you sooner. How may I help you?" or
"Thanks for being patient. What can I do for you?"

3. "I HOPE THIS WILL SOLVE YOUR PROBLEM."
"This will solve the problem," or
"Allow me to take care of the problem."

4. "I DON'T UNDERSTAND WHY CUSTOMER SERVICE DIDN'T HELP YOU."*
"I'm sorry there has been a misunderstanding. Please hold and I'll call customer service for you. Will that be all right?"

5. "ORDER PROCESSING HAS HAD A LOT OF PROBLEMS LATELY. I'LL CALL OVER THERE AND GET THIS STRAIGHTENED OUT FOR YOU."*
"I'll be pleased to call order processing for you and resolve your problem. Do you mind holding for a minute?"

6. "MR. KING IS IN A MEETING. WHY DON'T YOU CALL BACK IN AN HOUR?"
"Mr. King is unavailable right now. May I help you?" or
"Mr. King is away from his office at the moment. May I help you or would you prefer to leave a message?"

7. "I'M SORRY IT TOOK SO LONG. NOW WHAT DO YOU WANT?"
"I'm sorry that you had to wait. How may I help you?"

8. "I'M SORRY YOU HAD TO WAIT. OUR TELEPHONE OPERATORS ARE VERY SLOW."
"I'm sorry that you had to wait. How may I help you?" or
"I apologize for the delay. Normally our telephone attendants are speedy."

If you find yourself using negative words, phrases or sentences, you need to take corrective action. One simple idea is to write "POSITIVE WORDS ONLY" and tape it to your telephone. Every time you use the telephone it will serve as a reminder to communicate a positive response.

---

*Note: There are a variety of positive statements that can be made for statements 4 and 5. The correct rephrasing should include a positive action plan for the customer.

TELEPHONE TECHNIQUE EIGHTEEN: CLOSING THE CONVERSATION

When you finish your telephone conversation there are some appropriate and courteous statements that should always be made. You should:

1. Thank the customer for calling.
2. Let the customer know you appreciate his/her business.
3. Provide assurance that any promises will be fulfilled.
4. Leave the customer with a positive feeling.

SOME COURTEOUS CLOSING STATEMENT EXAMPLES:

"Thank you for calling. We appreciate your business."

"Thanks for your order."

"Feel free to call us anytime."

"I'm glad we were able to help."

"Goodbye and thanks for calling."

"I enjoyed talking with you."

"If you have any additional questions please call me."

Let the customer hang up first.

This is simple courtesy, plus it gives the caller a final chance to add something.

REVIEW OF SECTION II

Check those telephone techniques you feel comfortable with by marking the appropriate box with a ☑. Those that need more work should be reviewed and discussed with your supervisor.

TELEPHONE TECHNIQUES	DO WELL	NEEDS WORK
1. HANDLING THE TELEPHONE	☐	☐
2. YOUR VOICE INFLECTION	☐	☐
3. YOUR BEST VOICE	☐	☐
4. ADDRESSING THE CALLER	☐	☐
5. ANSWERING THE TELEPHONE	☐	☐
6. EFFECTIVE LISTENING	☐	☐
7. MANAGING OBJECTIONS	☐	☐
8. THE ART OF NEGOTIATION	☐	☐
9. THE SERVICE FOLLOW-UP CALL	☐	☐
10. ASKING QUESTIONS	☐	☐
11. MAKING THE OUTBOUND SERVICE CALL	☐	☐
12. DELIVERING BAD NEWS	☐	☐
13. MANAGING DIFFERENT CALLER BEHAVIORS	☐	☐
14. MANAGING YOUR VOICE MESSAGE SYSTEM	☐	☐
15. MANAGING TELEPHONE MESSAGES	☐	☐
16. MANAGING THE CUSTOMER CALLBACK	☐	☐
17. SOME STATEMENTS TO AVOID	☐	☐
18. CLOSING THE CONVERSATION	☐	☐

SECTION III

UNDERSTANDING CUSTOMER NEEDS

Now that you have learned some important telephone techniques, let's concentrate on the customer. Every customer has needs and expectations that must be met. To understand these needs, carefully complete the exercises and activities in this section.

On the following page is a conversation between Mike, an order taker, and his supervisor, Mary. Make note of how you would answer if your supervisor asked the same questions Mary is asking Mike.

UNDERSTANDING CUSTOMER NEEDS (Continued)

As a trainee in the order processing department of Amax, Inc., Mike's job is to answer customer telephone calls, provide price quotes and take orders. The job is hectic because of the number of calls received each day.

After a few weeks on the job, Mike's supervisor, Mary, met with him to discuss his job performance. Mary began the discussion with a question.

Mary: "Mike, how do you think you are doing?"

Mike: "Well, pretty good I think. There is still a lot to learn but I feel I am making progress."

Mary: "I agree. Your progress has been good. Let me ask you a question. How would you describe the responsibilities of your job?"

Mike: "My responsibilities include handling as many customer calls as possible, making sure my orders are accurate and knowing our products well."

Mary: "Those are all important responsibilities and you are doing a good job in those areas."

Mike: "Thanks."

Mary: "How do you think you are at providing good customer service?"

Mike: "I must be O.K. since I don't know of any customer complaints."

Mary: "I don't know of any complaints either, but what type of service do you think our customers want?"

Mike: "Well, I haven't thought much about it. I guess they want accurate orders and fast delivery. From what many tell me, they are not too happy with our delivery dates."

Mike has the potential to be a very good order processor and provider of quality customer service. Right now, however, Mike is like a lot of people in similar jobs. He is so busy handling customer calls that he has not had time to think about customer service.

When his supervisor asked him, "What type of service do you think your customers want?" Mike did not have a clear understanding of his customer's service needs.

WHAT YOUR CUSTOMER WANTS

To understand better what your customer wants, ''listen'' to three customers explain their needs.

Suppose you asked three of your customers, ''What are your service needs?'' Chances are you would hear statements similar to those that follow. As you read each response, LISTEN closely to what the customer has to say. Then write in the space provided what you think the customer wants.

CUSTOMER #1

''I want service I can depend on. When I call your company and have a question, I expect an answer. I don't want to be transferred from one person to another only to learn someone needs to call me back. I also expect correct information. If I receive incorrect information, it may cause me a lot of unnecessary work. For example, if you promise a delivery date, I want to depend on that information. When you don't do what you promised, it causes problems for me.''

WHAT DOES CUSTOMER #1 WANT?

CUSTOMER #1

1.

2.

3.

4.

WHAT YOUR CUSTOMER WANTS (Continued)

CUSTOMER #2

"When we decide to buy from a company, we consider everything: the product, the service and the price. Most companies have an 800 number. All promise wonderful service but sometimes I feel the only service is the 800 number. I want to speak with someone who knows what they are doing and can help me. We like consistency. We want to receive courteous, fast service from everyone with whom we speak. I hate callbacks. I know it is not possible for someone to help me immediately every time I call, but the majority of the time we should be able to get the information we need."

CUSTOMER #2 WANTS:

1.

2.

3.

4.

CUSTOMER #2 also mentioned three considerations they take into account when they decide to buy from a company.

WHAT WERE THEY?

1.

2.

3.

CUSTOMER #3

''My biggest complaint is people who don't listen. Sometimes it seems they are just going through the motions. If I call, and explain what I want, or what I think I want, they simply seem to record the information, quote a price and say goodbye. I'm sure there are times when suggestions could be offered to me about different alternatives. Customer service representatives should know their products and services better than I do. Another thing, I don't enjoy being put on hold. I often hear, ''Please hold for a second while I check that.'' Then, after what seems like an eternity, I hear a live voice again.''

CUSTOMER #3 WANTS:

1.

2.

3.

(Check your answer with the author on the next page)

WHAT YOUR CUSTOMER WANTS (Continued)

AUTHOR RESPONSES

CUSTOMER NEEDS AND WANTS

CUSTOMER #1 WANTS: (PAGE 47)

1. DEPENDABLE SERVICE
2. ANSWERS TO QUESTIONS
3. NOT TO BE TRANSFERRED FROM ONE PERSON TO ANOTHER
4. CORRECT INFORMATION

CUSTOMER # 2 WANTS: (PAGE 48)

1. TO TALK WITH SOMEONE WHO KNOWS WHAT THEY ARE DOING
2. CONSISTENT SERVICE
3. COURTEOUS SERVICE
4. A FAST RESPONSE

CUSTOMER #2 SAID: WHEN WE DECIDE TO BUY FROM A COMPANY WE CONSIDER:

1. THE PRODUCT
2. THE SERVICE
3. THE PRICE

CUSTOMER #3 SAID: (PAGE 49)

1. LISTEN
2. OFFER SUGGESTIONS
3. DON'T PUT ME ON HOLD

Having completed the exercise—answer this question:

ARE THE CUSTOMERS ASKING FOR TOO MUCH?

When you think about it, customers do ask for a lot. They expect a fast response, error-free information, quality products, courteous treatment, on-time shipments and much more.

CUSTOMER NEEDS

If you were the customer, would your needs be any different from those mentioned at the bottom of page 50? Wouldn't you expect quality service? If the company you called failed to provide what you wanted, wouldn't you do what most customers do; namely, find another company to do business with?

CUSTOMER NEED	CUSTOMER MEANING
1. LISTEN TO ME	PAY ATTENTION—UNDERSTAND ME—HEAR WHAT I HAVE TO SAY.
2. I WANT DEPENDABLE SERVICE	I NEED TO KNOW YOU WILL MEET YOUR COMMITMENTS.
3. GIVE ME CORRECT INFORMATION	DON'T GUESS AT THE RIGHT ANSWER—IF YOU DON'T KNOW OR HAVE TO CHECK, OKAY, BUT DON'T GIVE ME THE WRONG INFORMATION.
4. DO NOT TRANSFER ME FROM PERSON TO PERSON	CONNECT ME WITH THE RIGHT PERSON THE FIRST TIME. DON'T JUST GET RID OF ME. DON'T LEAVE ME ON HOLD.
5. KNOW YOUR JOB, HELP ME AND WHEN APPROPRIATE, OFFER SUGGESTIONS	I DEPEND ON YOUR KNOWLEDGE. PLEASE OFFER SUGGESTIONS OR COUNSEL ME.
6. I NEED CONSISTENT SERVICE	BE DEPENDABLE. TREAT ME LIKE THE IMPORTANT CUSTOMER I AM.
7. I EXPECT COURTEOUS SERVICE	LET ME KNOW YOU APPRECIATE MY BUSINESS EACH TIME I CALL.
8. I EXPECT ACTION	DON'T MAKE ME WAIT UNNECESSARILY. I KNOW YOU CAN'T ALWAYS MEET MY DEMANDS BUT BE AS RESPONSIVE AS POSSIBLE.

ATTITUDE IS YOUR KEY TO SUCCESS

We have talked about procedures thus far; however, perhaps the key factor to quality customer service is your ATTITUDE.*

ATTITUDE IS YOUR MENTAL POSITION ON FACTS—OR MORE SIMPLY, THE WAY YOU VIEW THINGS.

There are five important items about attitude that you should always remember.

1. YOUR ATTITUDE TOWARD CUSTOMERS INFLUENCES YOUR BEHAVIOR. YOU CANNOT ALWAYS CAMOUFLAGE HOW YOU FEEL.
2. YOUR ATTITUDE DETERMINES THE LEVEL OF YOUR JOB SATISFACTION.
3. YOUR ATTITUDE AFFECTS EVERYONE WHO COMES IN CONTACT WITH YOU, EITHER IN PERSON OR ON THE TELEPHONE.
4. YOUR ATTITUDE IS NOT ONLY REFLECTED BY YOUR TONE OF VOICE BUT ALSO BY THE WAY YOU STAND OR SIT, YOUR FACIAL EXPRESSION AND IN OTHER NONVERBAL WAYS.
5. YOUR ATTITUDE IS NOT FIXED. THE ATTITUDE YOU CHOOSE TO DISPLAY IS UP TO YOU.

Whenever you talk on the telephone you have a choice. You can reflect a positive, upbeat attitude, or you can make another, less desirable, choice.

It is not always easy to be positive. There are work situations that can have negative influences on your attitude. Someone you work with may depress your attitude, your workload may be heavy and produce stress, or certain customers can be demanding and even unpleasant to work with. All of these factors affect your attitude.

---

*For an outstanding book on attitude, order *Attitude: Your Most Priceless Possession,* from the order form in the back of the book.

You have probably had days that begin with your feeling great. As the day progresses, however, your feeling of well-being starts to slip away. By day's end, you are glad it is over.

If you have had this experience, you are normal. However, even on down days, you have some control. Your control begins when you decide that YOU are responsible for the attitude you display. When you decide to be positive and customer-oriented, you have taken the first step. Your challenge is to maintain this positive attitude despite situations that take place throughout the day.

For example, suppose your first telephone contact of the day is with a very unpleasant customer. This provides you with a choice. You can allow this unpleasant situation to affect your attitude negatively for the rest of the day, or you can put the incident behind you and consciously regain a positive attitude. Every daily activity provides another "attitude opportunity."

It sounds easy, doesn't it? Well, as you know, it is not always that easy. However, you also probably know that the benefits of a positive customer-oriented attitude outweigh the alternatives. For one thing, with a positive attitude your job satisfaction remains high, and you will continue to provide good customer service.

ATTITUDE IS YOUR KEY TO SUCCESS (Continued)

Following are some thoughts to help you establish and maintain a positive and customer-oriented attitude.

1. Start each day with thoughts about the positive aspects of your job.

2. When negative events occur, take a deep breath and re-establish a positive attitude by focusing on activities that allow you to regain your perspective.

3. Whenever possible, avoid people and situations that are predictably negative.

4. Share your attitude when things are going well. Attitudes are caught, not taught.

JAMES RECEIVED A POOR JOB PERFORMANCE REVIEW. HIS SUPERVISOR SAID HIS ATTITUDE TOWARD CUSTOMERS WAS THE BIGGEST PROBLEM. THIS TOOK JAMES BY SURPRISE BECAUSE HE WAS UNAWARE OF THE AFFECT HE WAS HAVING ON OTHERS.

JAMES DECIDED TO TRY TO IMPROVE HIS ATTITUDE. FIRST, HE MADE A LIST OF WHAT HE CONSIDERED TO BE NEGATIVE IMPACTS ON HIS ATTITUDE. AFTER REVIEWING THE LIST, JAMES REALIZED THAT WORKING WITH TWO OR THREE UNPLEASANT CUSTOMERS EACH DAY HAD A NEGATIVE INFLUENCE ON HIS ATTITUDE TOWARD ALL OF THE OTHERS. JAMES SUDDENLY REALIZED THAT ALTHOUGH HE TALKED WITH 30 CUSTOMERS A DAY, HE WAS ALLOWING A VERY SMALL PERCENTAGE OF THEM TO INFLUENCE HIS BEHAVIOR NEGATIVELY.

JAMES DECIDED TO IMPROVE HIS ATTITUDE BY REFLECTING ON CUSTOMER SUCCESSES HE HAD ALREADY EXPERIENCED FOLLOWING EACH UNPLEASANT CUSTOMER EXPERIENCE.

The facing page contains a customer service attitude survey. This should provide you with feedback about your attitude toward customers.

To check your customer service attitude, complete this survey. Answer each statement honestly.

(CIRCLE ONE)

1. T or F CUSTOMERS EXPECT TOO MUCH FROM ME.

2. T or F CUSTOMERS SHOULD TRY TO UNDERSTAND SOME OF OUR PROBLEMS.

3. T or F IT IS NOT REASONABLE FOR A CUSTOMER TO EXPECT A FAST RESPONSE ON EVERY CALL.

4. T or F CUSTOMERS ARE TOO DEPENDENT.

5. T or F CUSTOMERS SHOULD NOT MIND BEING PLACED ON HOLD FOR A MINUTE OR SO.

6. T or F IF CUSTOMERS KNEW HOW MANY CALLS I HANDLED EVERY DAY, THEY WOULD APPRECIATE ME MORE.

7. T or F CUSTOMERS SHOULD SHOW GREATER PATIENCE.

8. T or F CUSTOMERS SHOULD UNDERSTAND WHY WE CAN'T HELP THEM WHEN THEY FIRST CALL.

9. T or F CUSTOMERS ARE TOO QUICK TO ESCALATE PROBLEMS TO MY SUPERVISOR.

10. T or F MOST CUSTOMERS SHOULD TRY TO SOLVE THEIR OWN PROBLEMS BEFORE THEY CALL US.

GIVE YOURSELF 1 POINT FOR EACH FALSE ANSWER AND 2 POINTS FOR EACH TRUE ANSWER.

YOUR SCORE: ____

(Answers are on the next page)

ATTITUDE IS YOUR KEY TO SUCCESS (Continued)

All of the answers are FALSE. If you scored a perfect 10, congratulations. If you scored higher than 13, your customer service attitude could use some improvement.

Let's review why the answers are false.

Q1. Customers do expect a lot of service. As a provider of customer service, it is not your job to define your customer's needs, but to respond to those needs.

Q2. Why should the customer need to understand your problems? They are concerned with their own problems.

Q3. The customer feels it is reasonable. Customers call when their work involves your company. They do not want to wait.

Q4. Some customers become very dependent on companies they do business with. This is exactly what you want. Customers who feel comfortable calling you will become regulars.

Q5. Try this: look at the second hand on your watch, then close your eyes. Keep them closed unitl you think a minute has elapsed, then open them. More than likely you opened your eyes before the minute was up. A minute can be a long time.

Q6. The customer doesn't really care how busy you are. Customers want to feel important. When they call they expect your full attention.

Q7. Yes, They probably should. Impatience however comes with the territory.

Q8. A customer wants fast, courteous service. When they have to wait, they are not getting what they want. When callbacks are unavoidable arrange to call the customer at a specific time. Do everything possible to honor this commitment.

Q9. Some customers <u>are</u> too quick to talk to supervisors. When they ask to do so they are saying, "You are not meeting my needs and I want to talk with someone else." There will be times you cannot satisfy a customer. Discuss these situations with your supervisor to learn how they are to be handled.

Q10. Yes, some customers could avoid calling you if they tried to solve their own problems. But why should they? The customer's view is, "That's your job." Why spend time solving problems if there is a more simple way to get a solution? Be grateful when customers call.

QUALITY CUSTOMER SERVICE DEFINED

Thus far in Section III we have learned customers wants and needs and learned the importance of a positive attitude. Now let's see if you can define what good customer service is. Write your brief definition below.

TO ME, QUALITY CUSTOMER SERVICE MEANS: _____

_____

_____

_____

_____

_____

_____

_____

There are several acceptable definitions of quality customer service. However, one key phrase that should always be included in a definition is:

SATISFY CUSTOMER NEEDS

If you included this phrase (or one close to it), your answer is a good one. Following is the author's definition:

QUALITY CUSTOMER SERVICE SATISFIES CUSTOMER NEEDS (REAL OR PERCEIVED) IN A CONSISTENT AND DEPENDABLE MANNER.

Note the phrase "REAL or PERCEIVED." This is very important in understanding quality customer service. It is not your perception of how good the service is that counts. IT IS THE CUSTOMER'S PERCEPTION, and this is discussed in the next section of this book.

SECTION IV

MANAGING THE CUSTOMER'S PERCEPTION

The final section of this book is devoted to understanding and managing customer perceptions. These perceptions include how customers react to your attitude, your concern for their problems and the way you handle their questions or service requirements.

When you provide service over the telephone, you may speak with the same customer many times. Even though you have never met this person face to face, you probably have an idea of what he or she is like. You may even have a mental image of what a particular customer looks like. Customers are no different. They also have an image of you.

Think of your favorite radio personalities. If you see them in person or on television, they often do not look like you imagined they would. The personalities of their voices have created mental images for you. Radio broadcasters are professional people. They create the image they want you to have. When you provide quality customer service, you are doing the same thing.

Let's quickly review the definition of quality customer service.

GOOD CUSTOMER SERVICE: SATISFIES CUSTOMER NEEDS (REAL OR PERCEIVED) IN A CONSISTENT AND DEPENDABLE MANNER.

CASE STUDY: THE WHOLESALE WIDGET COMPANY

You are customer service manager of the Wholesale Widget Company. You believe customer service is good because there have been very few customer complaints. The company is profitable and sales have been increasing. Despite this, you feel a survey of customers would be worthwhile to learn their feelings about WWC's service. A few weeks ago, you mailed several hundred customer service questionnaires.

THE RESULTS WERE:

62% RATED YOUR CUSTOMER SERVICE "AVERAGE"

23% RATED IT "POOR"

13% RATED IT "GOOD"

2% RATED IT "EXCELLENT"

With these results, what attitude best reflects your thinking as customer service manager?

1. 77% of our customers rated our service as average or better. That's pretty good.
2. Our average customer is satisfied. Overall we need some improvement, but we are doing a pretty good job.
3. We have a serious problem. 23% of our customers rated our service as poor. We need to do something, and do it now!

A. Which statement reflects your view? ____ #1 ____ #2 or ____#3.

B. List three steps you will take to improve customer service.

1.
2.
3.

C. If this situation is not corrected, list three things that could happen to your company.

1.
2.
3.

TURN THE PAGE FOR THE ANSWERS

CASE STUDY: AUTHOR'S RESPONSE

A. WHICH STATEMENT REFLECTS YOUR VIEW?

The best answer is #3. We have a serious problem. Whenever customers are dissatisfied with service, something must be done. In this case, a very high percentage (23%) are dissatisfied. Before the survey you thought service was good. You were wrong. It is customers who decide how good the service is.

B. WHAT STEPS SHOULD BE TAKEN?

The first thing you need to do is find out why your customers are not satisfied. Next, a plan should be developed to address specific customer concerns. Finally, it will be necessary to implement and monitor this plan.

Your answer should be similar to the above. As customer service manager, you will need a method for customer feedback to insure your plan is working.

C. IF YOUR SERVICE SITUATION IS NOT CORRECTED, WHAT COULD HAPPEN TO THE COMPANY?

When customers are not satisfied, they will take their business elsewhere. Sales will fall and profits will tumble. Customers will mention their poor experience to others, and the reputation of the company will suffer. Ultimately there will be fewer jobs, smaller pay increases and less opportunity for all.

THE CUSTOMER'S PERCEPTION: AN EXERCISE

Following is a list of telephone statements that have been made to customers. Read each statement and rate the PERCEPTION you think a customer would have after hearing the statement. Rate each statement with a "G" if you think the customer reaction would be good and a "P" if you think it would be poor.

RATING

1. ____ GOOD MORNING, WHOLESALE WIDGET COMPANY, JIM SMITH SPEAKING. MAY I HELP YOU?
2. ____ SORRY, THAT'S NOT MY JOB...YOU WILL HAVE TO CALL THE ORDER PROCESSING DEPARTMENT.
3. ____ GOOD MORNING, WHOLESALE WIDGET.
4. ____ MRS. JONES IS OUT. ANY MESSAGE?
5. ____ THANKS FOR YOUR ORDER.
6. ____ I DON'T WORK IN THAT DEPARTMENT, SO I CAN'T HELP YOU.
7. ____ GOOD MORNING, CUSTOMER SERVICE.
8. ____ I REALLY DON'T KNOW WHY OUR SERVICE PERSON DIDN'T RETURN YOUR CALL. DID YOU TRY TO CALL THEM BACK?
9. ____ I'M SORRY IT TOOK SO LONG TO GET BACK TO YOU. I'M SURE WE CAN SOLVE YOUR PROBLEM WITH THIS CALL. NOW, HOW MAY I HELP YOU?
10. ____ MAY I REVIEW YOUR ORDER TO INSURE WE HAVE ALL OF THE INFORMATION?
11. ____ WHOM WERE YOU HOLDING FOR?
12. ____ THANKS FOR CALLING.
13. ____ MR. SMITH, I'M SORRY YOU RECEIVED THE WRONG MATERIAL, BUT I WROTE THE ORDER DOWN JUST AS YOU GAVE IT TO ME.

AUTHOR RESPONSE TO THE CUSTOMER'S PERCEPTION EXERCISE

1. **Good morning, Wholesale Widget Company, Jim Smith speaking. May I help you?**
   PERCEPTION RATING: GOOD. THE TELEPHONE WAS ANSWERED USING THE FOUR COURTESY POINTS.
   1. A GREETING **2.** STATEMENT OF COMPANY NAME
   3. THE PERSON'S NAME **4.** AN OFFER OF HELP
   If an incoming call has been previously answered at a central station, there is no need to restate the company name. In this case the department or group name should be used.

2. **Sorry, that's not my job...you will have to call the order processing department.**
   PERCEPTION RATING: POOR. THIS STATEMENT WILL ONLY FRUSTRATE THE CUSTOMER.

3. **Good morning, Wholesale Widget.**
   PERCEPTION RATING: POOR. IF A RECEPTIONIST MADE THIS STATEMENT, IT WOULD BE ACCEPTABLE IF AN OFFER TO HELP WERE INCLUDED. IN TELEPHONE SITUATIONS, WHERE A CALL IS ANSWERED AT A CENTRAL POINT AND THEN ROUTED TO THE REQUESTED INDIVIDUAL OR DEPARTMENT, THERE IS NO NEED FOR A PERSONAL INTRODUCTION. IN ALL OTHER CASES, HOWEVER, IT IS IMPORTANT TO LET THE CUSTOMER KNOW TO WHOM THEY ARE SPEAKING.

4. **Mrs. Jones is out. Any message?**
   PERCEPTION RATING: POOR. IF YOU CHANGE THE PHRASE TO: "MAY I TAKE A MESSAGE?" IT WOULD BE MORE ACCEPTABLE.

5. **Thanks for your order.**
   PERCEPTION RATING: GOOD. THIS SIMPLE STATEMENT SHOULD ALWAYS BE USED WHEN THE CUSTOMER PLACES AN ORDER.

6. **I don't work in that department, so I can't help you.**
   PERCEPTION RATING: POOR. EVEN THOUGH YOU DO NOT WORK IN THAT DEPARTMENT AND CANNOT HELP THE CUSTOMER, THERE IS NO EXCUSE FOR NOT OFFERING TO HELP BY TRANSFERRING THE CALL OR TAKING A MESSAGE.

7. **Good morning, customer service.**
   PERCEPTION RATING: POOR. TWO OF THE FOUR CUSTOMER ANSWERING COURTESY POINTS WERE OMITTED:
   1. INTRODUCING YOURSELF
   2. OFFERING TO HELP
8. **I really don't know why our service person didn't return your call. Did you try to call them back?**
   PERCEPTION RATING: POOR. TO PROVIDE GOOD SERVICE MEANS TAKING RESPONSIBILITY. THIS DOES NOT MEAN YOU HAVE TO PERSONALLY SOLVE THE CUSTOMER'S PROBLEM, BUT YOU NEED TO ASSURE THE CUSTOMER THAT CORRECTIVE ACTION WILL BE TAKEN.
9. **I'm sorry it took so long to get back to you. I'm sure we can solve your problem with this call. Now, how may I help you?**
   PERCEPTION RATING: GOOD. AN APOLOGY WAS MADE FOR SLOW SERVICE AND THE CUSTOMER RECEIVED ASSURANCE THAT THE PROBLEM WILL BE SOLVED.
10. **May I review your order to insure we have all the information?**
    PERCEPTION RATING: GOOD. ACCURACY IS IMPORTANT. TO REPEAT A CUSTOMER'S ORDER OR REQUEST IS A GOOD IDEA.
11. **Whom were you holding for?**
    PERCEPTION RATING: POOR. NOT KNOWING WHOM THE CUSTOMER IS HOLDING FOR IS A COMMON PROBLEM. WHEN THIS OCCURS, GET ON THE LINE AND SAY: "I'M SORRY, I HAVE FORGOTTEN WHOM YOU WERE HOLDING FOR." THEN WRITE THE PERSON'S NAME SO YOU WILL REMEMBER. WHENEVER POSSIBLE PROVIDE THE CALLER WITH A STATUS REPORT. FOR EXAMPLE: "SALLY IS STILL ON ANOTHER CALL. WOULD YOU LIKE TO CONTINUE TO HOLD OR MAY I TAKE YOUR NUMBER AND HAVE HER CALL YOU?" WHENEVER POSSIBLE GIVE THE CUSTOMER A CHOICE.
12. **Thanks for calling.**
    PERCEPTION RATING: GOOD. ALWAYS THANK A CUSTOMER FOR CALLING.
13. **Mr. Smith, I'm sorry you received the wrong material, but I wrote the order down just as you gave it to me.**
    PERCEPTION RATING: POOR. WHEN A MISUNDERSTANDING OR MISTAKE HAS OCCURRED, IT IS NOT IMPORTANT TO FIX BLAME FOR THE PROBLEM. THE IMPORTANT THING IS TO TAKE WHATEVER CORRECTIVE ACTION IS REQUIRED TO SATISFY THE CUSTOMER.

Every statement you make on a telephone to a customer carries with it a perception. Your objective is to manage this perception to insure there is customer satisfaction with the service your provide.

MANAGING THE CUSTOMER'S PERCEPTION: THE CUSTOMER SERVICE CALL

MARTHA: "Good Morning, Customer Service Department, Martha English speaking. May I help you?"

CUSTOMER: "This is Ken Taylor from AP Systems. I need to order some new valves for our engineering department."

MARTHA: "I'll be glad to handle that for you. What type do you need?"

CUSTOMER: "Well, the engineering department said they needed either the 516 or the 311 model. I'm not sure which one is the best. Is there a price difference?"

MARTHA: "Yes, there is a 50 cent difference. The 516 is less expensive. How many valves do you need?"

CUSTOMER: "We need 85."

MARTHA: "Do you mind holding while I work up a price quote?"

CUSTOMER: "No, go right ahead."

MARTHA: "Thanks for holding. The price on the 516 is $2.00 per valve. The 311's are $2.50 each. Your total cost for the 516 would be $170.00, and $212.50 for the 311. Would you like me to explain the difference between the two models?"

CUSTOMER: "Yes, please do."

MARTHA: "The 516 is our newer design. It is stronger and a little smaller than the 311. I think the last time your company ordered they purchased the 516. Would you like me to check on that?"

CUSTOMER: "Yes, would you please."

MARTHA: "Sure. Do you mind holding for a moment?"

CUSTOMER: "No."

MARTHA: "I'll be right back."

MARTHA: "Thanks for holding. Your last order was in June and you ordered the 516."

CUSTOMER: "I had better double check with engineering. I will have to call you right back."

MARTHA: "If you like I'll hold while you call them. Will that be okay?"

CUSTOMER: "Sure, I'll be right back."

CUSTOMER: "I'm glad I checked. They want the 311."

MARTHA: "So that will be 85 311 valves. Is the billing and shipping address the same as your last order?"

CUSTOMER: "Yes, it is."

MARTHA: "Good, we will get the shipment out this afternoon and you can expect delivery on Friday. Will that be all right?"

CUSTOMER: "Yes, that's fine."

MARTHA: "Is there anything else I can do for you?"

CUSTOMER: "No, that should do it."

MARTHA: "Thanks for your order."

CUSTOMER: "You're welcome. Goodbye."

MARTHA: "Goodbye."

In this telephone contact Martha provided the customer with excellent service. The customer appeared unsure about which valve to order. Martha helped by explaining the differences, by checking on a previous order and then holding while her customer checked with engineering. Martha was patient and offered every assistance she could.

Let's examine a few of Martha's statements to see the customer perception they provided.

MANAGING THE CUSTOMER PERCEPTION (Continued)

MARTHA'S STATEMENTS	CUSTOMER'S PERCEPTION
"Good morning, Order Processing Department, Martha English speaking. How may I help you?"	SHE IS FRIENDLY AND WANTS TO HELP US.
"Do you mind holding while I work up a price quote?"	SHE IS COURTEOUS.
"I think the last time your company ordered, they purchased the 516. Would you like me to check that for you?"	SHE IS OFFERING HER ASSISTANCE.
"Do you mind holding for a few seconds?"	SHE ASKS PERMISSION BEFORE PLACING THE CUSTOMER ON HOLD.
"If you want, I'll hold while you call them (engineering). Will that be all right?	SHE IS CONCERNED—WANTS TO HELP—PROVIDES COURTEOUS SERVICE
"Is there anything else I can do for you?"	SHE OFFERS ADDITIONAL HELP.
"Thanks for your order."	SHE APPRECIATES MY BUSINESS.

Suppose you were the customer. What do you think your perception of Martha and her company would be? How would you rate the customer service she provided? Check each statement below that you think her customer Ken Taylor would agree with.

1. ___ I can depend on their service.
2. ___ I received a fast response.
3. ___ I can trust their service.
4. ___ Martha was very helpful.
5. ___ She listened to me.
6. ___ I was counseled.
7. ___ I received courteous service.
8. ___ The information was accurate.
9. ___ She understood my problem.
10. ___ I can rely on them.

Ken probably would have checked all of the statements. In one simple telephone conversation the needs of the customer were completely met.

TELEPHONE SERVICE SKILLS INVENTORY

The kind of service you provide is up to you. If your objective is to become a professional customer service provider, two things must be done. First you need to assess your present skill level to determine where improvement is needed. Next you need to develop a personal action plan to improve your skills. These steps can be done using this page and the action plan on page 66, with the help of your supervisor.

Following is a service skills inventory. Grade yourself on each skill area. Use a rating of "A" if you feel you are excellent at the particular skill, "B" for good and "C" if you need improvement. Ask your supervisor to provide his/her opinion on your self-scored assessments.

SERVICE

____ I accept responsibility for providing customer service.
____ I understand the importance of quality service.
____ I know what our customers want and need.
____ I satisfy customers by understanding their needs and doing my job well.
____ I realize that a positive customer perception of our service is essential.
____ I am customer-oriented.
____ I have a positive attitude.

TELEPHONE TECHNIQUES I know how to:

____ handle the telephone and use all of its features.
____ extend courtesy on every call.
____ address the caller.
____ transmit a positive attitude.
____ answer calls using the four courtesies.
____ listen to distinguish between statements, objections and questions.
____ manage objections.
____ ask questions. (I know how and when to use open and closed questions and can question to determine problems and requests.)
____ make outbound calls.
____ deliver bad news. (I can use the two techniques.)
____ recognize and manage caller behavior. (I know how to manage the aggressive and assertive callers.)
____ arrange customer callbacks. (I always make and keep commitments.)
____ avoid using statements that will create the wrong customer perception.

Develop a personal action plan for better service on the next page.

YOUR ACTION PLAN FOR BETTER SERVICE

Your personal action plan will be developed in four steps:

STEP 1. List all skill areas you rated as "B" or "C."

_____

_____

_____

_____

_____

STEP 2. Identify your five most critical skill areas that need improvement.

1. _____ 2. _____ 3. _____

4. _____ 5. _____

STEP 3. Write down an action plan to improve the five skills. Include specific activities and dates you plan to start and complete (use a separate piece of paper for this step).

SKILL AREA	IMPROVEMENT ACTIVITY	START	COMPLETE
1.			
2.			
3.			
4.			
5.			

STEP 4: Review Steps 1, 2 and 3 with your supervisor and commit to a date to review progress on your action plan.

Once you have made progress with the first five skill areas, you can develop an action plan for any remaining skill areas rated "B" or "C." Maintain a personal action plan until you rate an "A" in each skill area. When your ratings are all "A's" you have reached your objective of becoming a provider of quality customer service. Make a commitment to yourself to become a professional. Good luck!

NOTES

FOR OTHER FIFTY-MINUTE SELF-STUDY BOOKS
SEE THE BACK OF THIS BOOK.

NOTES

FOR OTHER FIFTY-MINUTE SELF-STUDY BOOKS
SEE THE BACK OF THIS BOOK.

NOTES

FOR OTHER FIFTY-MINUTE SELF-STUDY BOOKS
SEE THE BACK OF THIS BOOK.

NOTES

FOR OTHER FIFTY-MINUTE SELF-STUDY BOOKS
SEE THE BACK OF THIS BOOK.

ABOUT THE FIFTY-MINUTE SERIES

We hope you enjoyed this book and found it valuable. If so, we have good news for you. This title is part of the best selling ***FIFTY-MINUTE Series*** of books. All other books are similar in size and identical in price. Several books are supported with a training video. These are identified by the symbol Ⓥ next to the title.

Since the first ***FIFTY-MINUTE*** book appeared in 1986, more than five million copies have been sold worldwide. Each book was developed with the reader in mind. The result is a concise, high quality module written in a positive, readable self-study format.

FIFTY-MINUTE Books and Videos are available from your distributor or from Crisp Publications, Inc., 95 First Street, Los Altos, CA 94022. A free current catalog is available on request.

The complete list of ***FIFTY-MINUTE Series*** Books and Videos are listed on the following pages and organized by general subject area.

MANAGEMENT TRAINING

	Self-Managing Teams	00-0
	Delegating for Results	008-6
	Successful Negotiation — Revised	09-2
Ⓥ	Increasing Employee Productivity	10-8
	Personal Performance Contracts — Revised	12-2
Ⓥ	Team Building — Revised	16-5
Ⓥ	Effective Meeting Skills	33-5
Ⓥ	An Honest Day's Work: Motivating Employees	39-4
Ⓥ	Managing Disagreement Constructively	41-6
	Learning To Lead	43-4
Ⓥ	The Fifty-Minute Supervisor — 2/e	58-0
Ⓥ	Leadership Skills for Women	62-9
Ⓥ	Coaching & Counseling	68-8
	Ethics in Business	69-6
	Understanding Organizational Change	71-8

MANAGEMENT TRAINING (Cont.)

	Project Management	75-0
	Risk Taking	076-9
	Managing Organizational Change	80-7
V	Working Together in a Multi-Cultural Organization	85-8
	Selecting And Working With Consultants	87-4
	Empowerment	096-5
	Managing for Commitment	099-X
	Rate Your Skills as a Manager	101-5

PERSONNEL/HUMAN RESOURCES

V	Your First Thirty Days: A Professional Image in a New Job	003-5
	Office Management: A Guide to Productivity	005-1
	Men and Women: Partners at Work	009-4
	Effective Performance Appraisals — Revised	11-4
	Quality Interviewing — Revised	13-0
	Personal Counseling	14-9
	Giving and Receiving Criticism	023-X
	Attacking Absenteeism	042-6
	New Employee Orientation	46-7
	Professional Excellence for Secretaries	52-1
	Guide to Affirmative Action	54-8
	Writing a Human Resources Manual	70-X
	Downsizing Without Disaster	081-7
	Winning at Human Relations	86-6
	High Performance Hiring	088-4

COMMUNICATIONS

	Technical Writing in the Corporate World	004-3
V	Effective Presentation Skills	24-6
V	Better Business Writing — Revised	25-4
V	The Business of Listening	34-3
	Writing Fitness	35-1
	The Art of Communicating	45-9
	Technical Presentation Skills	55-6
V	Making Humor Work	61-0
	50 One Minute Tips to Better Communication	071-X
	Speed-Reading in Business	78-5
	Influencing Others	84-X

PERSONAL IMPROVEMENT

V	Attitude: Your Most Priceless Possession — Revised	011-6
V	Personal Time Management	22-X
	Successful Self-Management	26-2
	Business Etiquette And Professionalism	32-9
V	Balancing Home & Career — Revised	35-3
V	Developing Positive Assertiveness	38-6
	The Telephone and Time Management	53-X
	Memory Skills in Business	56-4
	Developing Self-Esteem	66-1
	Managing Personal Change	74-2
	Finding Your Purpose	072-8
	Concentration!	073-6
	Plan Your Work/Work Your Plan!	078-7
	Stop Procrastinating: Get To Work!	88-2
	12 Steps to Self-Improvement	102-3

CREATIVITY

	Systematic Problem Solving & Decision Making	63-7
V	Creativity in Business	67-X
	Intuitive Decision Making	098-1

TRAINING

	Training Managers to Train	43-2
	Visual Aids in Business	77-7
	Developing Instructional Design	076-0
	Training Methods That Work	082-5

WELLNESS

V	Mental Fitness: A Guide to Stress Management	15-7
	Wellness in the Workplace	020-5
	Personal Wellness	21-3
	Preventing Job Burnout	23-8
V	Job Performance and Chemical Dependency	27-0
	Overcoming Anxiety	29-9
	Productivity at the Workstation	41-8
	Health Strategies for Working Women	079-5

CUSTOMER SERVICE/SALES TRAINING

	Sales Training Basics — Revised	02-5
	Restaurant Server's Guide — Revised	08-4
	Effective Sales Management	31-0
	Professional Selling	42-4
	Telemarketing Basics	60-2
	Telephone Courtesy & Customer Service — Revised	64-7

CUSTOMER SERVICE/SALES TRAINING (CONT.)

V	Calming Upset Customers	65-3
V	Quality at Work	72-6
	Managing Quality Customer Service	83-1
	Customer Satisfaction — Revised	84-1
V	Quality Customer Service — Revised	95-5

SMALL BUSINESS/FINANCIAL PLANNING

Consulting for Success	006-X
Understanding Financial Statements	22-1
Marketing Your Consulting or Professional Services	40-8
Starting Your New Business	44-0
Direct Mail Magic	075-2
Credits & Collections	080-9
Publicity Power	82-3
Writing & Implementing Your Marketing Plan	083-3
Personal Financial Fitness — Revised	89-0
Financial Planning With Employee Benefits	90-4

ADULT LITERACY/BASIC LEARNING

Returning to Learning: Getting Your G.E.D.	02-7
Study Skills Strategies — Revised	05-X
The College Experience	07-8
Basic Business Math	24-8
Becoming an Effective Tutor	28-0
Reading Improvement	086-8
Introduction to Microcomputers	087-6
Clear Writing	094-9
Building Blocks of Business Writing	095-7
Language, Customs & Protocol For Foreign Students	097-3

CAREER BUILDING

Career Discovery - Revised	07-6
Effective Networking	30-2
Preparing for Your Interview	33-7
Plan B: Protecting Your Career	48-3
I Got The Job! - Revised	59-9
Job Search That Works	105-8

To order books/videos from the FIFTY-MINUTE Series, please:

1. **CONTACT YOUR DISTRIBUTOR**

   or

2. **Write to Crisp Publications, Inc.**
   95 First Street **(415) 949-4888 - phone**
   Los Altos, CA 94022 **(415) 949-1610 - FAX**